Open-Ended Questions COACH

Read, Think, Write, Assess, Improve

D

Margaret C. Moran

Open-Ended Questions Coach, Level D: Read, Think, Write, Assess, Improve
57NA
ISBN# **1-58620-533-1**

EVP, Publisher: Steven Zweig
Managing Editor: Kelly Bellini
Creative Director: Spencer Brinker
Art Director: Farzana Razak
Developmental Editor: Leslie Patterson
Production Manager: Michelle McGuinness
Contributing Authors: Lida Lim, Maurice O'Flynn, and Lesli J. Favor, Ph.D.
Contributing Editor: Heidi Sheehan

Interior Design: Janet Yuen
Cover Design: Farzana Razak
Cover Photo Credit: Matthew Klein/Corbis

Triumph Learning 333 East 38th Street, New York, NY 10016-2777

A Haights Cross Communications company

Printed in the United States of America.

10 9 8 7 6 5 4 3 2

Table of Contents

Part A

Unit III Answering Questions That Ask for an Opinion

Part A

Introduction

Welcome to the smart way to write answers to open-ended questions!

Some students will read a question on a test and just start writing. They won't stop to think and plan. They may not even make sure they know what the question is asking.

Don't be like these students. Learn to use the smart way to answer open-ended questions:

Read • Think • Write • Assess • Improve

Let's look at each step.

1 **READ** the question thoughtfully. Look for key words like *describe, explain, main idea*. This will help you understand what you need to do.

2 **THINK** about what the reading says. Then think about what the question asks you to write about the reading.

3 **WRITE** down some ideas to answer the question while you brainstorm. Think about how to put these ideas together. Then write your answer.

4 **ASSESS** what you have written. This means to read your writing and see how you might improve it. Ask yourself how you might make your answer better.

5 **IMPROVE** your writing. Revise and rewrite your answer as needed to answer the question more *clearly*, *accurately*, and *completely*.

These 5 steps may seem like a lot of work. But once you learn the steps, you will find them very easy to use. This book will help you practice them. After a while, you will not even have to think about them. They will just come naturally to you. You will say to yourself, "Here's an open-ended question. What does the question ask me to do?" And you are on your way to applying these 5 steps.

As you will see, these steps work for *any type of open-ended test question*. It doesn't matter whether you have to write a short answer or a long answer. These 5 steps work for all kinds of selections and answers.

HINT: To help you remember the steps, put out 5 fingers. Name each finger with a step. Your thumb is "read," and so on. If you forget a step, put out your fingers and see if you can name each finger.

Answering Questions That Ask You for Information

Unit 1

Lesson 1

Summarizing the Main Idea and Supporting Details

- The **main idea** tells what a piece of writing is mainly about.
- The **supporting details** add information about the main idea.

Open-ended test questions are sometimes based on the main idea and supporting details. The question may not say "main idea and supporting details," but you have to use them to answer the question.

For example, a question may ask you to write about what a selection is *mainly about*. Or a question may ask you to write a *summary*. You cannot answer either question without finding the main idea and supporting details.

How do you find the main idea?

1. Read the title.
   - The title often suggests the main idea.
2. Look for the **topic sentence**.
   - The topic sentence is usually in the first paragraph. The topic sentence states the main idea.
3. To be sure, read the entire piece to see what it is mainly about.

How do you find the supporting details?

1. Read the selection and figure out the main idea.
2. Look for details that support the main idea.
   - Supporting details describe, explain, or provide interesting information about the main idea.

In this Lesson, you will learn how to...

- answer a question that asks you for the main idea and supporting details.
- write complete sentences.

The National Cherry Blossom Festival

Every spring, people come from all over the world to Washington, D.C., for the National Cherry Blossom Festival. That's when the city's cherry trees bloom. There are thousands of these trees planted across the city near most of the monuments. When the trees bloom, Washington, D.C., is a sea of pink and white flowers. But the blossoms last only a few weeks.

There weren't always cherry trees in Washington, D.C. There weren't even cherry trees in the United States until about 100 years ago. In 1912, Japan presented 3,022 cherry trees as a gift to the United States. They were planted in Washington, D.C. Some are still standing.

In 1935, Washington, D.C., held the first festival to celebrate the planting of the trees. The festival lasted a week and included a parade. From that year on, the festival became an annual event. In 1948, the National Cherry Blossom Festival held a contest to name a Cherry Blossom Queen. The queen was chosen from 50 "princesses." Each young woman represented one of the 50 states. Since then, the National Cherry Blossom Festival chooses a queen every year. The queen and the princesses ride in the Cherry Blossom Parade. The parade also has floats, huge balloons, and marching bands.

Besides watching the parade, there are many other things to do during the festival. Visitors can go to the annual tree-planting ceremony. During the ceremony, more cherry trees are planted across the city. Visitors can also stroll through the street fair. There, they can see Japanese crafts, listen to music, and try different types of food. Every year the Capital Children's Museum teaches children how to create cherry blossoms out of tissue paper.

In 1994, Washington, D.C., extended the festival from one week to two weeks. The city couldn't fit all the activities into one week. This is proof that the festival is a popular spring event.

STEP 1 **READ** *the question thoughtfully.*

Read the question carefully.

Identify the main idea of the article. Use information from the article to support your answer.

1. What are you supposed to do?

   Underline the parts of the question that tell you what to do. These are your key words. They give you instructions.

2. **Write the key words here.**

   ____

   ____

   ____

3. Now check yourself to be sure you understand the instructions.

   Restate the question in your own words.

   ____

   ____

   ____

   ____

4. Do the question and what you just wrote agree?

   Circle *yes* or *no*.

5. If your answer is no, try again. Reread the question.

   Write the key words again.

   ____

   Restate the question in your own words.

   ____

   ____

STEP 2 THINK

THINK about what the reading says.

1. What is the title of the article?

   Write it here.

   ____

2. What is the main idea of the article?

   Write the sentence in the first paragraph that states the main idea of the article.

   ____

   ____

   ____

3. Find as many important details from the article as you can. You want to look for the most important details that describe the main idea.

   Write those details here.

   ____

   ____

   ____

   ____

   ____

   ____

THINK about what the question asks you to do.

4. You are summarizing the main idea and the supporting details. Make sure you know which details are supporting details.

   Write the supporting details here.

   ____

   ____

   ____

5. Think about the details you wrote to answer number 3 in this step. Choose the most important details that describe the main idea.

   Circle those details in number 3 that you want to use in your answer.

HINT: ***Some details are more important than others. Try to find the most important details to use in your answer. You have a limited amount of space to write in.***

STEP 3 WRITE

1. Look at the answers you wrote for numbers 1 and 2 in Step 2. Use that information to write a topic sentence for your answer.

   Complete the following sentence:

   The main idea of the selection is ____________________

   ____

   ____

HINT: ***One way to create a topic sentence is to repeat some of the key words from the question.***

2. **Write the circled details from number 3 in Step 2 in the order that you want to use them.**

   ____

   ____

   ____

   ____

   ____

   ____

3. **Pull your ideas together and write your answer.**

STEP 4 ASSESS *what you have written.*

How do you know if you have written a clear, complete, and correct answer? One way is to check your answer against a rubric. A rubric is a guide that lists things to look for in a piece of writing. The teachers who will assess your answers will be using rubrics. See how they do it by using this rubric to assess your answer.

4 = I state the main idea correctly and clearly.
I state the details clearly. The details support, or explain, the main idea.
I write complete sentences.

3 = I state the main idea correctly and clearly.
I include some details that are stated clearly.
I write complete sentences.

2 = I state the main idea but not clearly.
I include a few supporting details, but they are not stated clearly.
I do not write complete sentences.

1 = I do not state the main idea correctly.
I include details that do not support the main idea.
I do not write complete sentences.

To help you use the rubric, let's look at Jelani's paper. It earned a "4".

The main idea of the article is that every year there is a National Cherry Blossom Festival in Washington, D.C. The first festival was in 1935. It lasted a week and had a parade. It celebrated the gift of cherry trees from Japan. In 1948, a Cherry Blossom Queen was crowned for the first time. There are so many things to do that the festival is two weeks now. People can go to a fair or parade, listen to music, eat food, plant more cherry trees, and much more. People come from all over the world for the festival.

What should you notice about Jelani's answer?

- ✔ He must have read the question carefully because he answered it completely and clearly.
- ✔ He repeats key words from the question in his topic sentence.
- ✔ He supports his answer with important details from the article.
- ✔ He writes complete sentences.

1. **Write Jelani's topic sentence here.**

____

____

2. How many of Jelani's sentences have important details that support the main idea?

   Write the number here. ____________

3. **Write one of the sentences with an important detail.**

____

____

Skill: Writing Complete Sentences

Because Jelani uses **complete sentences**, his answer reads smoothly. It is also easy to understand.

- A sentence is a group of words that expresses a complete thought.
- A sentence contains a *subject* and a *predicate*.
  - The subject tells who or what the sentence is about.
  - The predicate tells what the subject does or is.

4a. What does the phrase *complete thought* mean? Look at the four groups of words below.

Circle the ones that are sentences.

- The trees swaying in the breeze.
- Children play in the grass.
- Hot dogs sizzling on the grill.
- There is a picnic.

Two of these groups of words are sentences. Two of these groups of words are just groups of words.

- They are incomplete sentences.
- They do not express a complete thought.
- They do not have subjects and predicates.
- They are called fragments.

4b. **Rewrite those two groups of words as sentences.**

____

____

How does your answer compare to Jelani's?

5. Did you repeat part of the question in your topic sentence? If you did, that's good.

   If not, try rewriting your topic sentence using keywords from the question.

   ____

   ____

6. Jelani used five important details to support his topic sentence.

   How many sentences did you use? ______________

7. If you used fewer than five important details, could you add to make your answer more complete?

   Write those details here.

   ____

   ____

   ____

   ____

   ____

8. Did you use any incomplete sentences in your answer? Reread your answer to see if you need to rewrite any sentences.

   If you need to rewrite any sentences, underline them.

IMPROVE *your answer.*

1. Think about the ideas you wrote about your answer.
2. Read the rubric on page 14 again. Think about your answer and about the description of the "4" paper.
3. **Use your new ideas to revise and rewrite your answer.**

Read the questions in "One Last Look" on the next page. These questions give you one last chance to polish your answer.

ONE LAST LOOK

Did you

- ❑ answer the question that was asked?
- ❑ include details to make your answer interesting and complete?
- ❑ write complete sentences?
- ❑ fill all or most of the answer lines?
- ❑ check your spelling and punctuation?

Lesson 2

More About Summarizing the Main Idea and Supporting Details

On a test, you might be asked to write a summary. A **summary** is a brief retelling of a longer piece of writing. To write a summary, you must include the

- **main idea** of what you are summarizing.
- most important **supporting details.**

You will usually find the main idea in the first paragraph of a longer piece of writing. It is the topic sentence. Remember that the main idea tells what the piece of writing is mainly about.

The rest of the paragraphs supply the supporting details. Supporting details add information about the main idea. When you write a summary, you should use only the most important supporting details. Do not include less important details and descriptions.

Remember, a summary
- restates the main idea.
- is much shorter than what you are summarizing.
- does **NOT** include minor details or descriptions.
- does **NOT** include your own opinions and ideas.

In this Lesson, you will learn how to...

- answer a question that asks you for a summary.
- select the most important information to include in a summary.
- revise run-on sentences.

INVENTING THE PERSONAL COMPUTER

There was a time not so long ago when people did not have computers in their homes. There were none in schools either. This may seem hard to believe, but it is true. The personal computer was not invented until the 1970s.

Before that, the only computers were huge machines called mainframes. They had to be kept in special dust-free rooms at certain temperatures. Instead of working on a keyboard in front of a screen, people punched holes in cards. The holes represented numbers and letters. The cards were fed into the mainframes and information came out. A person could not just sit down in front of a mainframe and begin typing a letter to a friend.

The first personal computer was called the Altair. It was created in 1974. This computer came in a kit that people had to assemble. Few people wanted to bother putting the Altair together.

In 1977, two men invented a computer that could be sent to people already assembled. It was called the Apple. Steve Wozniak and Steven Jobs created their computer in the Jobs' garage. The computer was one piece with a plastic case and a screen. It looked like a small television and it had a keyboard. A person could sit down in front of the screen and type out a letter. Wozniak and Jobs started to advertise their computer, and people began to buy it. By 1980, the men had to move out of the garage. There were so many orders that they hired 1,000 people to make and ship their computers.

In 1981, a company called IBM started selling its own personal computer. It was called the IBM PC. IBM worked with a company called Microsoft to create software programs to run on its computers. Many people began buying IBM PCs. Like Apple computers, they were fast and easy to use.

Since then, personal computers have gotten even smaller, faster, and cheaper. In 1984, Jobs and Wozniak introduced the Macintosh computer. It looked much like the computers you use today. It had windows on the computer screen, a mouse, and pictures you could click on. When other companies saw the number of personal computers being sold, they began building and selling them, too. Each company wanted people to buy its computers. As a result, companies worked on making their computers better than the competition. Companies also reduced prices. Once, a desktop computer like the ones you have in school cost $2,500 or more. Today, a new computer may cost around $600.

STEP 1 READ *the question thoughtfully.*

Read the question carefully.

Write a paragraph briefly summarizing the reading selection.

1. What are you supposed to do?

   Underline the parts of the question that tell you what to do. These are your key words.

2. **Write those key words here.**

   ____

   ____

3. On page 20 you read a definition of a summary.

   Write that definition here.

   ____

   ____

4. Make sure you understand what the question asks you to do.

   Restate the question in your own words.

   ____

   ____

STEP 2

THINK

THINK about what the reading says.

1. What is the title of the reading selection?

   Write the title here.

   ____

2. What is the main idea of the article?

   Write the main idea here.

   ____

   ____

Before you choose any details, read and complete the following boxes. They will help you choose the most important details for your summary.

Skill: Choosing Important Details

There are many details in this article about computers. However, the directions on page 20, tell you to choose the most important details. How do you know what the most important details are?

3a. How many paragraphs are there in the article?

Write the number of paragraphs here.______________

3b. Each paragraph has a main idea. These main ideas will be the supporting details for your summary.

Write those main ideas here.

1. ______________________________________

____

2. ______________________________________

____

3. ______________________________________

____

4. ______________________________________

____

5. ______________________________________

____

6. ______________________________________

____

3c. **Write the main idea of the article again.**

____

____

3d. Now read each sentence you wrote in question 3b. Ask yourself: Does this sentence have information that is *needed* to tell what the article is about?

Circle each sentence that has information you need to tell what the article is about. Cross out the sentences you do *not* need.

Be sure to put the information from the circled sentences into your summary.

When you are writing a summary, always look for the main idea of each paragraph. These are the main points that you should include in your summary. They become your supporting details in your answer.

THINK about what the question asks you to do.

4. Before you write your answer, it is smart to think about the question again. You want to be sure you know what to do.

   Write what you have to do to answer the question.

WRITE

1. **Write the definition of a summary here.**

2. Now organize your ideas.

   Number the ideas you selected in Step 2 from 1 to 6 in the order you want to use them.

3. **Now write your summary.**

ASSESS *what you have written.*

Now exchange what you have written with a classmate. Use the following rubric to help you assess your classmate's answer. As you do this, think about how this answer is different from yours.

4 = I state the main idea of the article clearly and correctly.
I use main points and only these points as my supporting details.
I state the main points clearly and correctly.
I write complete sentences.

3 = I state the main idea of the article clearly and correctly.
I use most of the main points as my supporting details.
I state the main points clearly and correctly.
I include minor details that should not be part of a summary.
I write complete sentences.

2 = I state the main idea of the article but not clearly.
I use only half the main points as my supporting details.
I clearly state the main points that I used.
I include minor details that should not be part of a summary.
I do not write complete sentences.

1 = I do not state the main idea of the article.
Most of the details I include are not main points.
I do not write complete sentences.

How does your classmate's answer measure up to the rubric? Let's look at a "2" response.

I like personal computers. The first one was called Altair. They are small. They are not like the big mainframes. They do not cost as much now. They used to cost $2,500 now they cost $600. Do you like computers?

What do you think about Raymond's answer?

- He did not understand the definition of a summary.
- He wrote a topic sentence that does not match the article well.
- He included details that were not main points.
- He added his own opinion.
- He did not write complete sentences.
- He did not write to fill all or most of the answer lines.

1. Raymond could improve his answer by first identifying the main idea of the entire article. What main idea should he have identified?

   Write the main idea of the article here.

2. Raymond's topic sentence does not match the article well.

   Explain to Raymond why his topic sentence does not match the article.

3. Raymond does not include important points in his summary. He includes only a few minor ones.

   Help Raymond by writing two main points from the article.

4. Raymond includes his own opinion. A writer of a summary should not add his or her own ideas to the summary.

   Write the sentence in which Raymond adds his opinion.

5. Raymond starts many sentences with the word *they*. Sometimes it is not clear what he means by the word *they*.

   Rewrite the following two sentences to make them clearer.

   They are small. They are not like the big mainframes.

Skill: Revising Run-on Sentences

Raymond also used a run-on sentence. A run-on sentence is one that is missing a punctuation mark or a connecting word like *and* or *but*. Raymond wrote the following:

They used to cost $2,500 now they cost $600.

These are really two complete thoughts, so they should be separated by a punctuation mark or a connecting word. There could be a period between *$2,500* and *now*.

They used to cost $2,500. Now they cost $600.

Or, there could be the connecting word *but* between $2,500 and *now*.

They used to cost $2,500, but now they cost $600.

6. Correct these run-on sentences. Choose one of the following four words for each sentence: *and*, *so*, *but*, *because*

HINT: ***Use a comma before these four words when you correct the sentences.***

Rewrite each run-on sentence with a connecting word.

6a. The cars collided the street was icy.

____

6b. The basketball player scored 55 points the fans roared.

____

6c. The city park was closed the game was at the high school.

____

6d. The day was sunny rain was in the forecast for the evening.

____

When you revise your answer, make sure you do not have any run-on sentences.

You have given Raymond and your classmate help to improve their answers. Now, let's look at your answer and see how you did.

7. Are you satisfied with your topic sentence?

   If not, rewrite it here.

   ____

   ____

   ____

8. There is one main point, or idea, in each paragraph. You should have the most important points in your answer.

   How many main points do you have?____________

9. **If you think you need to add more main points, write them here.**

   ____

   ____

   ____

   ____

   ____

   ____

10. A summary should not include descriptions and minor details. Have you included any descriptions and minor details?

    Cross out any descriptions and minor details in your answer.

    These should be taken out when you improve your answer.

11. A summary should not include your own opinion. Have you included any of your own ideas or opinions?

    Put brackets around any of your own ideas or opinions in your answer.

    These should be removed when you improve your answer.

12. Reread your answer to check your sentences. Have you written any run-on sentences?

    Underline any run-on sentences in your answer.

    You will need to correct these when you revise your answer.

IMPROVE *your answer.*

1. Think about the ideas you have written about your answer.
2. Read the rubric again. Pay particular attention to the description of the "4" paper.
3. **Use all your ideas to revise and rewrite your answer.**

Remember to review the "One Last Look" questions on the next page!

ONE LAST LOOK

Did you

- ❑ answer the question that was asked?
- ❑ include details to make your answer interesting and complete?
- ❑ write complete sentences?
- ❑ fill all or most of the answer lines?
- ❑ check your spelling and punctuation?

Lesson 3

Describing a Personal Experience

You may be asked on a test to describe a personal experience. A **personal experience** is anything that you did or saw. It could be going to a party, playing a sport, winning an award, acting in a play, or getting a pet. Your answer must be interesting and clearly stated.

How do you write a description of a personal experience? First, you have to decide what to write about. That is your main idea. You will turn that into your topic sentence. Then you have to remember details about the experience. Those will be the supporting details for your answer.

To help you plan your answer, you need to remember:

- what happened
- who was involved
- where it took place
- when it took place
- why it took place
- how the experience turned out

Transition words help connect ideas and sentences. Some transition words like *then* and *now* show **time order**. This means the order in which something happened. Time-order words can help make your writing clear.

In this Lesson, you will learn how to...

- answer a question that asks you to describe a personal experience.
- use transition words that show time order to make your writing clear.

MY MYSTERY TRIP

Dad and I had an adventure last weekend. I was eating breakfast Saturday morning when Dad came into the kitchen. "I have a surprise for you!" he said.

The spoon fell out of my hand. "A surprise?" I asked suspiciously. Was it cleaning my room? "What surprise, Dad?"

"We're going on a trip. You'll love it!" he grinned.

I picked up my spoon and went back to my cereal. I don't like trips. I like to stay home. "Where are we going?" I asked. I popped a spoonful of cereal in my mouth.

"It's a mystery," Dad said. "I'll help you pack your suitcase. Each thing you pack will be a clue. You can use the clues to solve the mystery."

"A mystery trip," I said. Even though I don't like trips, I was interested.

In my bedroom we pulled out an old red suitcase. "First, you need to pack some sunglasses," Dad said.

"Sunglasses?" I said. "People wear sunglasses at the beach. Are we going to Seashell Beach?"

"No!" said Dad. He grinned. "Second, pack some paper and colored pencils."

I thought about that. Then I said, "Dad, you know I like to draw animals and trees. Are we going someplace outdoors like the zoo?"

Dad laughed. "Yes, it is outdoors. It's not the zoo! Next, pack your hiking boots."

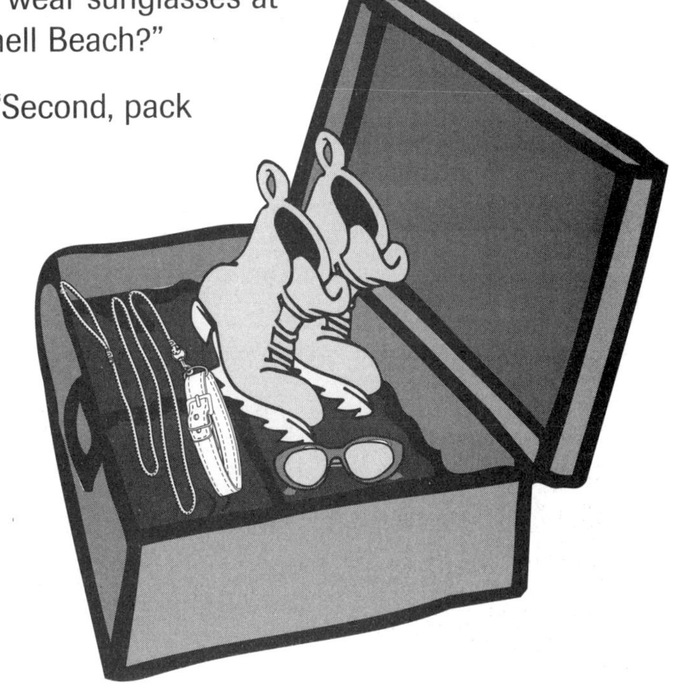

"Hiking boots!" I shouted. "Dad, you gave it away. We're going hiking!"

"But *where* are we going hiking?" Dad asked.

I thought hard. Where was a sunny place to hike?

Dad gave one more clue. "Last, pack Snappy's leash." Snappy is our dog.

"We're going hiking with Snappy!" I said. "The trails in Redrock Park are sunny and fun to draw. We can hike with Snappy on the trails, and I can sketch from Redtop Rock!"

Then I thought a moment. "Dad," I said, "One clue you gave me wasn't right."

"Which one?" he said.

"The suitcase," I said. "Redrock Park is across town. We don't need to pack a suitcase to travel there."

Dad smiled and popped sunglasses on his nose. "You are too smart for me. I guess that clue was unfair. But it didn't stop you for long, did it?"

"No," I agreed. I popped sunglasses on my own nose. "Let's get Snappy and go on our trip!"

STEP 1 **READ** *the question thoughtfully.*

Read the question carefully.

The writer, his dad, and his dog were going on a hike. Write about a personal experience that was mysterious, exciting, funny, or embarrassing. Include as many details as you can.

1. What are you being asked to do?

   Underline those parts of the question that tell you what to do. These are the key words in the question.

2. **Write the key words here.**

   ____

   ____

   ____

3. Check that you understand what the question asks you to do.

   Restate the question in your own words.

   ____

   ____

   ____

STEP 2 THINK

THINK about what the reading says.

1. What is the main idea of the story?

   Write the main idea.

   ____

   ____

Did the writer remember to answer the what, who, where, when, why, and how of the personal experience? Answer the planning questions to decide.

2. ***What*** **happened?**

   ____

3. ***Who*** **was involved?**

   ____

4. ***Where*** **did it happen?**

   ____

5. ***When*** **did it happen?**

   ____

6. ***Why*** **did it happen?**

   ____

7. ***How*** **did it turn out?**

   ____

THINK about what the question asks you to do.

8. **Write the key words from the question again.**

____

____

____

9. What kind of experience are you going to describe?

   Circle your choice.

   mysterious ***exciting*** ***funny*** ***embarrassing***

10. What is the experience you want to write about?

    Write the experience here.

____

____

____

WRITE

1. Use what you want to write about as your topic sentence.

   Write your topic sentence here.

____

____

Brainstorm ideas for your description. Answer these five planning questions. They will be your supporting details.

2. ***Who* was involved?**

3. ***When* did it happen?**

4. ***Where* did it happen?**

5. ***Why* did it happen?**

6. ***How* did it turn out?**

7. Think about the experience you are going to write about. Reread your details in numbers 2 through 6.

   Add details if you think you need more information.

HINT: ***The more information you brainstorm, the easier it will be to write 14 lines.***

8. Now organize your ideas.

Write your supporting details in the order you want to use them.

1. ______________________________

   ____

2. ______________________________

   ____

3. ______________________________

   ____

4. ______________________________

   ____

5. ______________________________

   ____

9. **Now write your answer.**

HINT: ***Be sure to write complete sentences. Complete sentences need a subject (doer) and a predicate (what was done).***

ASSESS *what you have written.*

How does your answer measure up to the rubric?

4 = I state the main idea of the experience clearly.
I include supporting details that answer all the planning questions.
I use transition words correctly and effectively.
I write complete sentences.

3 = I state the main idea of the experience clearly.
I include answers to most of the planning questions.
I use some transition words.
I write complete sentences.

2 = I state the main idea of the experience, but it is not clear.
I include the answers to a few of the planning questions.
I do not use transition words.
I do not write complete sentences.

1 = I do not state the main idea of the experience.
I do not use the planning questions in writing my answer.
I do not use any time-order words.
I do not write complete sentences.

What score would you give yourself? Before you decide, let's look at a "4" paper.

My most embarrassing experience happened last Fourth of July. The Becerras were at our house for a barbecue. The grown-ups were in the backyard. The little kids were running all over playing tag. My mom was in the kitchen. I asked her if I could help. She told me to carry the big bowl of potato salad out to the picnic table. First, I got out the back door with the bowl. Next, I got down the steps with the bowl. Then I tripped over a little kid. The bowl of potato salad went flying. It landed right in Mrs. Becerra's lap. She started to scream. I ran and got a towel. I tried to wipe off the potato salad. It only smeared it worse. Mrs. Becerra had to go home and change her clothes. I was so embarrassed.

What do you think of Brianna's answer?

- ✓ She must have read the question carefully because she wrote about what it asked.
- ✓ She states in the first sentence what she is writing about—an embarrassing experience.
- ✓ She answers the planning questions.
- ✓ She uses time-order words, so her answer reads smoothly.

Let's take a closer look at Brianna's answer to see why it earned a "4".

1. Brianna identifies her main idea in her topic sentence.

   Write Brianna's topic sentence.

   ____

   ____

Brianna answers these planning questions.

2. ***Who* is involved?**

   ____

3. ***When* does it take place?**

   ____

4. ***Where* does the experience take place?**

   ____

5. ***Why* does it take place?**

   ____

   ____

   ____

6. ***How* does it turn out?**

   ____

   ____

Did you notice that Brianna uses a lot of description? She helps you see what was happening. These extra details make the answer more interesting.

7. **Write one sentence from her answer that tells you what was happening in Brianna's yard.**

____

____

Skill: Using Transitions: Time-Order Words

Brianna's answer reads smoothly because she uses transition words. Transition words help to connect one sentence or idea to the next. This makes reading the piece smoother.

Brianna chose transition words that show time order. She thought it was important to describe the order in which the disasters happened.

The following is a list of some useful transition words for you to know. They all help show the order of things.

before, after
first, second, third, fourth,
then, now
yesterday, today, tomorrow
then, next
soon, later
last, finally

8a. Brianna uses three transition words in her description of the events that caused her to lose hold of the bowl.

Write the three words here.

____

8b. Reread the story on page 35. The writer uses transition words.

Number the things the boy packed in the order he packed them. Write the number on the first line before each phrase.

- ___ ___________ **Snappy's leash**
- ___ ___________ **sunglasses**
- ___ ___________ **hiking boots**
- ___ ___________ **some paper and colored pencils**

8c. **On the second line, write the time-order word from the story that tells you the correct order.**

When you revise your answer, see if time-order words will make it easier to understand.

How does your answer compare to Brianna's answer?

9. Did you state clearly what kind of experience you had?

If not, rewrite your topic sentence so it more clearly states the type of experience—mysterious, exciting, funny, or embarrassing.

____

____

10. Did you include the what, who, when, where, why, and how?

If not, write what you forgot here.

11. Did you write any description that would help the reader see what happened to you? If not, what details can you add that describe what happened?

Write those details here.

12. Did you use any time-order words? Would some transition words help your answer read more smoothly?

Circle the place or places in your answer where you could add a transition.

IMPROVE *your answer.*

1. Think about the ideas you have written about your answer.
2. Read the rubric again. Think about your answer and the description of the "4" paper.
3. **Use all your ideas to revise and rewrite your answer.**

Remember to review the "One Last Look" questions on the next page!

ONE LAST LOOK

Did you

- ❑ answer the question that was asked?
- ❑ include details to make your answer interesting and complete?
- ❑ write complete sentences?
- ❑ fill all or most of the answer lines?
- ❑ check your spelling and punctuation?

Answering Questions That Ask You to Explain

Unit 11

Lesson 4

Comparing and Contrasting Information

A test question might ask you to explain the similarities or the differences among people, things, or ideas. Such a question is asking you to compare and contrast. When you **compare** you show how things are alike. When you **contrast** you show how things are different.

To write a compare and contrast answer, you must
- show how the things are similar and how they are different.
- select at least two similarities and two differences to write about.
- find details in the reading that show those similarities and differences.

Creating a table or diagram can help you organize your information before you write. This kind of special table or diagram is called a **graphic organizer**.

Using transition words to show that you are comparing or contrasting can make your answers more interesting. These words can also make your answer read more smoothly. **Transitions** are words that act like bridges to connect ideas and sentences.

In this Lesson, you will learn how to...

- answer a question that asks you to compare two things.
- use a graphic organizer to organize your information.
- use transition words to add interest to your writing.

WHALES AND SHARKS

Two of the most interesting creatures in the ocean are sharks and whales. At first glance, they may seem to be very much alike. They both live in the ocean. They both swim and have fins. But they have few other things in common. Whales and sharks are very different.

For example, whales have tails that lie flat. If you took an x-ray of the whale's tail you would see that it has bones. Touch a whale's skin and it will feel smooth and rubbery. Even though whales look like big fish, they are mammals like humans. Whales are the largest mammals on earth. Like other mammals, whales have lungs and must hold their breath to go under water. But instead of a nose, whales have a blowhole on top of their head. It opens and closes to let air in and out. Whales have to keep their blowhole closed when they dive. Otherwise water will get into their lungs.

In comparison, shark tails are upright. They are made of a tough but bendable tissue called cartilage. Your ears are made of cartilage. To see what cartilage feels like, take a hold of your ear and bend it. If you touch a shark's skin, it will feel rough. That is because sharks have scales, like fish. In fact, sharks are the biggest fish in the sea. Unlike whales, sharks do not need to go to the water's surface for air. Instead, sharks have gills, like other fish. The gills allow oxygen from the water to enter the shark's body.

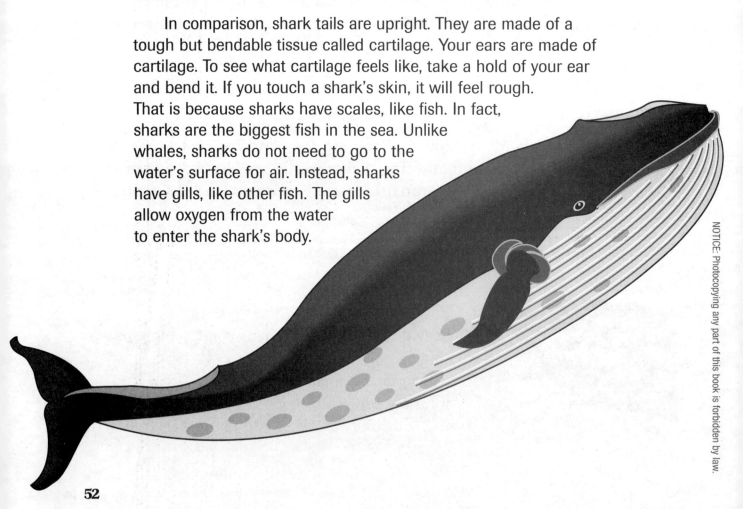

One of the most amazing things about sharks is their sense of smell. Some scientists think that most of the shark's brain is used for smelling. Smell is how sharks find their food. They can smell blood almost a quarter-mile away. That is as long as four football fields. On the other hand, whales do not have a sense of smell. They find their food through hearing and sight. Both whales and sharks have excellent hearing.

Whales and sharks eat the same things: fish and other sea creatures. Sharks sometimes attack other sharks for food. Whales do not usually bother other whales. Neither whales nor sharks attack human beings often. Even so, it is wise to stay out of the water if a shark or whale is nearby.

As you can see, whales and sharks are very different creatures. They share the same oceans, but they do not have much else in common.

STEP 1

READ *the question thoughtfully.*

Read the question carefully.

Explain three similarities and three differences between whales and sharks. Use information from the article to support your answer.

1. Do you understand what you are supposed to do?

   Underline those parts of the question that tell you what you are to do.

2. **Write the key words here.**

   ____

   ____

3. Always check to be sure that you understand what the question wants you to do.

   Restate the question. Start your answer with the words

   I have to ______________________________________

   ____

   ____

HINT: ***Always check to be sure that your restatement agrees with the question.***

STEP 2 **THINK**

THINK about what the reading says.

Skill: Organizing Information by Using a Chart

The article contains a great deal of information about whales and sharks. How can you write about it all? How can you keep it all straight? One way is to organize the information in a chart. This is also known as a **graphic organizer**.

1a. Look at the chart below. It is an example of a graphic organizer. It has a title and two columns. One column is labeled **Whales** and the other is labeled **Sharks**. The title is *Comparing Whales and Sharks*. This means the chart should be filled in with *similarities* between the two columns. The first row of this chart has already been filled in. Read the article again. Try to find all the qualities whales and sharks share.

Fill in rows 2–6 with similarities.

Comparing Whales and Sharks	
Whales	**Sharks**
1. live in the ocean	1. live in the ocean
2.	2.
3.	3.
4.	4.
5.	5.
6.	6.

This chart is titled *Contrasting Whales and Sharks*. This means the chart should be used to list *differences* between the two columns. This chart already has the first row filled in. Reread the article. Try to find all the differences between whales and sharks.

Fill in rows 2–6 with differences.

Contrasting Whales and Sharks	
Whales	**Sharks**
1. mammal	1. fish
2.	2.
3.	3.
4.	4.
5.	5.
6.	6.

Look at both charts. Now you have the information you need for your answer.

THINK about what the question asks you to do.

2. **Write the key words again.**

____

____

3. **How many similarities do you need to write about?** __________

4. **How many differences do you need to write about?** __________

5. Think about the key words and the details you used to fill the charts. Go back to your graphic organizers.

   Circle the similarities and differences you want to write about. Remember that you must choose pairs.

6. You should include some description about each similarity and difference you chose to put in your answer. For example, the article says:

   - Whales are "mammals like humans."
   - Sharks are "the biggest fish in the sea."

   Do not just list the similarities and differences in your answer. Try to describe them. Go back to the article and reread the similarities and differences you circled.

   On the following lines, write some description from the article for each pair of similarities and differences.

   This difference is ____

   ____

   This difference is ____

   ____

   This difference is ____

   ____

This similarity is

___

This similarity is

___

This similarity is

___

HINT: ***The more information you have before you begin to write, the better your answer will be.***

STEP 3 WRITE

1. **Restate what you are supposed to do.**

___

2. Turn this into a topic sentence for your answer.

Write a topic sentence here.

___

3. Go back to the descriptions of similarities and differences you chose in Step 2. Decide which set you want to write about first in your answer. Whichever you choose, you should talk about all three similarities together and all three differences together. Do not mix up the similarities and the differences.

   Number the similarities and the differences in the order you want to use them in your answer.

4. **Now write your answer.**

STEP 4 ASSESS *what you have written.*

Now exchange what you have written with a classmate. How would you rate his or her answer based on this rubric?

4 = I state the main idea clearly.
I include three similarities and three differences.
These are mostly followed by description.
They are not just listed.
I use transitions to make my answer read more smoothly.
I write complete sentences.

3 = I state the main idea clearly.
I include three similarities and three differences.
These are generally stated correctly and followed by some description.
I use a few transitions.
I write complete sentences.

2 = I state the main idea although not clearly.
I do not include all three similarities and three differences.
I just list them with little or no description.
I do not use transitions. My answer is choppy to read.
I do not write complete sentences.

1 = I do not state the main idea clearly.
I write about only one or two similarities and/or differences.
I include no description.
My answer is choppy and does not read smoothly.
I do not write complete sentences.

Before evaluating your classmate's answer, let's look at a "3" paper.

Whales and sharks both live in the ocean, but they are very different. They both use fins to move through the water. Both whales and sharks have a very good sense of sound. Their good hearing helps them find food. I am surprised at how different they are. I know a whale is a mammal unlike a shark. A shark is a fish. A whale needs oxygen from the air to breathe. That is why whales have lungs. A shark gets its oxygen from water through its gills. Whales have flat tails. Sharks have upright tails. Are you surprised at how different whales and sharks are?

What do you notice about Tiyana's answer that earned it a "3" and not a "4"?

- ✔ She has a topic sentence that has some of the key words from the question.
- ✔ She includes some description from the article to make her answer interesting to read.
- ✔ She uses a few transition words, so parts of her answer read smoothly.
- ✔ She writes complete sentences.

Tiyana's answer has a few problems.

- Her topic sentence could be much clearer.
- She did not list all of the similarities together.
- She could have used more transition words.

1. What do you notice about Tiyana's topic sentence? She does not restate the question in her topic sentence.

   Write Tiyana's topic sentence here.

   ____

   ____

2. Tiyana's topic sentence is interesting, but not completely clear. Can you rewrite it to include more of the key words?

   Write a new topic sentence for Tiyana.

   ____

   ____

   ____

3. Tiyana did not list all her similarities together. This makes her answer harder to understand. Look back at Tiyana's answer and find the information she needs to move.

   Put brackets around the information about the first similarity in Tiyana's paper.

4. Let's look at what is good about Tiyana's answer. Did you notice that she restates information from the article in her own words? For example, the article says:

> Instead, sharks have gills, like other fish. The gills allow oxygen from the water to enter the shark's body.

Write the sentence that Tiyana wrote about how sharks get oxygen.

____

____

5. Look at your classmate's paper. Did he or she write about sharks, gills, and oxygen?

If so, write the sentence or sentences here. If not, write your own sentence or two about sharks, gills, and oxygen here.

____

____

____

6. How does your classmate's sentence or sentences compare to Tiyana's sentence about sharks, gills, and oxygen?

Write your comparison of the answer here.

____

____

____

____

HINT: ***It is important to include description from whatever you are writing about. Description means information. BUT you need to restate the description in your own words.***

Skill: Using Transitions: Compare and Contrast Words

Most of Tiyana's answer is easy to read and understand. One reason is that Tiyana uses transition words that show comparison and contrast. Look at the lists of compare and contrast transition words.

Similarities

alike, as, like, same as, similar to, both

Differences

although, but, different, however, though, unlike

7a. Tiyana uses compare and contrast transition words in her answer.

Circle all the compare and contrast transition words in Tiyana's answer.

7b. Tiyana should have used a contrast word to connect the two sentences below.

Whales have flat tails. Sharks have upright tails.

Help make Tiyana's answer smoother and clearer. Combine Tiyana's two sentences into one sentence. Connect the two thoughts with a contrast transition word.

Write your sentence here.

Now look at your own answer and see how it compares to Tiyana's.

8. Did you repeat some of the key words to create your topic sentence? If yes, that is great.

   If not, try rewriting your topic sentence using some of the key words.

   ____

   ____

   ____

9. Tiyana uses three similarities and three pairs of differences in her answer. Did you?

   Circle *yes* or *no*.

10. If you used fewer than three similarities and three pairs of differences, what could you add? Go back to the charts on page 55 and 56. Find additional similarities and or additional pairs of differences that you could use in your answer.

    Write the similarities and/or differences here.

    ____

    ____

    ____

    ____

11. Are there any places in your answer where you could add description?

    Underline any places where you could add description.

12. Did you use any compare or contrast transition words in your answer?

    Circle *yes* or *no*.

    If not, look at the lists on page 64 to see which words you might add to your answer.

STEP 5 IMPROVE *your answer.*

1. Think about the ideas you have written about your answer.
2. Read the rubric again. Pay particular attention to the description of the "4" paper.
3. **Use all your ideas, as well as any ideas your classmate added, to revise and rewrite your answer.**

Remember to review the "One Last Look" questions on the next page!

ONE LAST LOOK

Did you

- ❑ answer the question that was asked?
- ❑ include details to make your answer interesting and complete?
- ❑ write complete sentences?
- ❑ fill all or most of the answer lines?
- ❑ check your spelling and punctuation?

Lesson 5

Explaining Cause and Effect

Sometimes you may be asked to write about why something happened. You have to read the article or story and look for what happened. Then you have to find out what caused it. In other words, you are looking for the **cause** and **effect** of some action or event. The **cause** is why something happened. The **effect** is what happened as a result.

Look at the following example:

George left his skates on the stairs. My dad tripped and fell.

What *happened*?

- George left his skates on the stairs. My dad tripped and fell.

What is the *cause*?

- George left his skates on the stairs.

What is the *effect*?

- My dad tripped and fell.

To explain cause and effect,

- identify the cause or causes of an event.
- add enough supporting details to make the cause clear to the reader.
- describe what the effect or the result was.

One way to make cause-and-effect relationships clear is by using transition words that show cause and effect.

In this Lesson, you will learn how to...

- answer a question that asks about cause and effect.
- use cause-and-effect transition words.

ALL ABOUT CLOUDS

Sometimes clouds look like puffy pieces of cotton. Before a thunderstorm, the clouds may look like dirty cotton. At other times, clouds stretch out long and thin across the sky. Whatever their shape, it often seems as though clouds are solid. But clouds are not solid. In fact, if you have ever flown in an airplane, you probably flew right through the middle of clouds. If you have ever walked or driven through fog, you were moving through clouds.

How Do Clouds Form?

Clouds consist of water droplets, ice crystals, or a mix of both.

First, water evaporates from the earth's surface. Oceans, lakes, rivers, and streams all have a part in making clouds. Water from these sources evaporates into the air. This means the water escapes into the air as a gas or vapor.

Next, the air cools. The cool temperature makes the vapor form into droplets, or tiny drops. The droplets form around tiny specks of solid material in the air. For example, over the ocean, a droplet may form around a speck of salt. Over a city, droplets form around specks of pollution such as ash from fires. The droplets group together to form clouds.

Clouds that form over oceans are "cleaner" than the ones over cities. Cities send up more pollution into the air, so there are more specks of solid material in city clouds. Some people say the air smells clean after a rain. Their sense of smell tells them that specks of pollution in the air have been washed out of it.

What Happens to Clouds?

The air can hold only so much water vapor. Cold air holds less water vapor than warm air. When too much water vapor collects, the air has to release it. The water droplets in clouds fall to earth as rain, sleet, or snow. When this happens, the water flows back into the lakes and streams, keeping them full.

STEP 1 READ *the question thoughtfully.*

Read the question carefully.

Explain what causes clouds to form and then release rain, sleet, and snow. Use information from the article for your answer.

1. What does it ask you to do?

   Underline the words that tell you what to do. These are the key words.

2. **Write the key words here.**

   ____

   ____

3. Check yourself to be sure you understand the question.

   Complete the following sentence.

   I am supposed to ________________________________

   ____

   ____

STEP 2 THINK

THINK about what the reading says.

1. What is the main idea of the reading?

   Write the main idea here.

   ____

2. **Write as many important details as you can find in the reading to explain the main idea.**

   ____

   ____

   ____

   ____

   ____

   ____

   ____

THINK about what the question asks you to do.

3. The question asks you to explain the causes of *two different effects.*

   Write the two effects here.

   ____

   ____

   ____

4. Think about the two effects and the details you have written in number 2.

   What is the cause or causes of the two effects?

   ____

   ____

   ____

5. Choose the details from number 2 that will help you explain these causes and effects.

   Circle those details.

STEP 3 WRITE

1. **Write a topic sentence for your explanation.**

   ____

   ____

   ____

HINT: ***Remember that the topic sentence should state your main idea.***

2. **Write the details (causes) from Step 2 in the order you want to use them.**

3. **Now write your answer.**

STEP 4 ASSESS *what you have written.*

What score would you give your answer?

4 = I state the main idea (effects) clearly.
I include the causes stated in the article.
I state the causes clearly and correctly.
I write complete sentences.

3 = I state the main idea (effects) clearly.
I include the causes stated in the article.
I generally state the causes correctly.
I write complete sentences.

2 = I state the main idea (effects) but not clearly.
I include some of the causes stated in the article.
I write complete sentences.

1 = I do not state the main idea (effects) correctly.
I do not include the causes stated in the article.
I do not write complete sentences.

Before evaluating your answer, let's look at a "4" paper.

How do clouds form and then rain, sleet, and snow?

Clouds are formed by groups of water droplets, ice crystals, or a mix of both. Water evaporates into the air from the earth. Then the air cools. It turns into drops of water. The drops form around specks like salt from the ocean. Pollution from cities causes drops to form, too. The air can hold only so much water vapor. It rains because the clouds have too much water vapor. It could sleet or snow, too.

What do you think about Esperanza's answer?

- ✔ She must have read the question carefully because she answered it completely.
- ✔ Her topic sentence states the effects clearly.
- ✔ She includes the causes accurately that are stated in the article.
- ✔ She uses description to make her answer interesting.
- ✔ She uses only important details for her description.
- ✔ She has written complete sentences.

Let's take a closer look at Esperanza's answer to see why it earns a "4".

1. Esperanza makes sure she focuses on what she is supposed to write about. She begins with a clearly stated topic sentence.

   Write Esperanza's topic sentence here.

   ____

   ____

HINT: ***Did you notice that Esperanza uses a question as her topic sentence? You don't always have to begin with a statement. You may use a question now and then for variety.***

2. Esperanza states very clearly in five sentences how clouds form.

   Write any two of those sentences here.

   ____

   ____

   ____

   ____

3. She describes what happens if there is too much moisture in clouds.

   Write those two sentences here.

   ____

   ____

   ____

   ____

4. In the following sentence from Esperanza's answer, there is a cause and effect.

   It rains because the clouds have too much water vapor.

   Circle the *effect*.

Skill: Using Transitions: Cause-and-Effect Words

One reason Esperanza's answer is clear is because she uses transition words. **Transition words** are bridges that connect sentences and ideas. Some transition words help to show cause and effect.

Cause-and-Effect Words

as a result, because, so, therefore

5a. **Find the cause-and-effect words in these sentences. Circle them.**

- The school was closed for winter break, so the computer club couldn't meet.
- Because of the lack of rain, the city fountains were turned off.
- The basketball court was closed for the night. As a result, the team had nowhere to practice.

5b. **Try rewriting these sentences to use a cause and effect transition word.**

- Ms. Ryan was looking for the principal. He was wanted in the office.
- The principal was wanted in the office. Ms. Ryan was looking for him.

It is time to look at your answer. How does it compare to Esperanza's answer?

6. Did you include any key words from the question in your topic sentence?

   If not, try to rewrite your topic sentence to include some key words.

7. Esperanza carefully chose information from the article to support her topic sentence. Do the details you selected explain your topic sentence? If not, what details can you add?

   Write the details here.

   ____

   ____

   ____

8. **Underline the sentences you wrote to explain what causes clouds to form.**

   Compare your sentences with Esperanza's. Do your sentences explain the cause completely and accurately?

9. **If not, circle the parts of your answer that you need to rewrite.**

10. **Underline the sentences you wrote to explain what causes clouds to release rain, sleet, and snow.**

    Compare your sentences about the cause of rain, sleet, and snow with Esperanza's. Do your sentences explain the cause completely and accurately?

11. **If not, circle the parts of your answer that you need to rewrite.**

12. Did you use any cause and effect transition words? Would adding any make your answer easier to understand?

    Put brackets around the sentence or sentences where you would like to add a transition.

IMPROVE *your answer.*

1. Think about the ideas you have written down about your answer.
2. Read the rubric again. Will your new ideas give you a "4" paper?
3. **Use your new ideas to revise and rewrite your answer.**

ONE LAST LOOK

Did you

- ❏ answer the question that was asked?
- ❏ include details to make your answer interesting and complete?
- ❏ write complete sentences?
- ❏ fill all or most of the answer lines?
- ❏ check your spelling and punctuation?

Lesson 6

Explaining Steps in a Process

How do you make a hot fudge sundae? You might not realize it, but there are steps to making a hot fudge sundae. What if you put the whipped cream on the bottom instead of the top?

One kind of question you might find on a test asks how to do something or make something. In your answer, you need to explain the steps for making or doing whatever is asked. You have to be sure you explain the steps in the right order.

When you are explaining steps in a process, you have to

- identify what you are making (the main idea).
- select information (supporting details) that will make your directions clear and complete.
- organize the supporting details in the order the steps need to be done.
- use transition words that show time order.

You should also use descriptive details. A **descriptive detail** is a detail that describes the main idea and supporting details more exactly and clearly. Descriptive details are not main points, but they should still be important to the topic. Using descriptive details makes your answer clear and more interesting.

In this Lesson, you will learn how to...

- answer a question that asks you to explain how to do something.
- use descriptive details to improve your answer.

Anasazi Pottery

The Anasazi (ah-nah-SAW-zee) were a people who lived long ago in what is today the southwestern United States. They lived in an area we call the Four Corners. Here, the four states of Colorado, New Mexico, Arizona, and Utah touch. The Anasazi lived in stone apartments that they built in the sides of cliffs. Experts have learned a great deal about these people from their pottery. Along with their cliff home, their pottery is all that we have left of the Anasazi. Women were the potters. They created pottery by using the "coil and scrape" method. To make pottery, the Anasazi needed four things: clay, sand, water, and fire.

1. First, the potter mixed water into clay to wet it. She made sure the clay was soft enough to work with, but not soggy.

2. Next, the potter added sand to the clay. Sometimes, instead of sand, she used crushed rocks or crushed pieces of pottery. The sand, rock, or pottery kept the clay from cracking when it dried.

3. The clay mix was then ready to shape into a pot, jar, bowl, or other item. The potter rolled pieces of clay into round strips, like rope. The length of the strips would determine how large the item would be. Then she made a circle with the first loop and laid the strips on top of each other in coils. A coil is a series of loops, like a spiral. The potter pinched the edges of the coiled layers together.

4. After that, the potter scraped the coils with a shell or piece of pottery. This made the surface of the item smooth. Sometimes the potter decorated the clay item with little dents made with her fingers.

5. At this point, the clay was still soft. It needed to be hardened so it could hold water or food. To do this, the potter "fired" it. Firing it meant baking it. This made the clay hard and strong.

6. As a final step, potters sometimes painted the outside of fired pottery. They made black or red paint from plants and minerals. Popular designs were triangles, thin lines, dots, and thick bands. After the paint dried, the pottery was ready to use. It could hold grain, meat, and even water.

STEP 1 **READ** *the question thoughtfully.*

Read the question carefully.

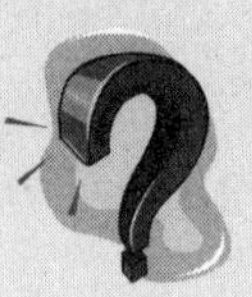

Suppose you are going to write a report about Anasazi pottery based on the information in this article. Your report will be divided into three headings: making the clay, shaping the clay, and firing the clay. Tell what information you would include under each heading.

1. What are you supposed to do?

   Underline those parts of the question that tell you what to do. These are your key words.

2. **Write the key words here.**

   ____

   ____

   ____

3. Be sure you understand what the question wants you to do.

   Restate the question in your own words.

   ____

   ____

   ____

   ____

STEP 2 THINK

THINK about what the reading says.

1. What is the article mainly about?

   Write the main idea of the article here.

   ____

   ____

2. The article begins with an introductory paragraph. Is there anything in the introduction that you might want to use in your report?

   Write that information here.

   ____

   ____

   ____

   ____

HINT: ***Look for details that have to do with the main idea of the article.***

3. How many steps are described in making the clay?

   Write the number here. ____________

4. **Write the steps for making the clay.**

____

____

____

____

5. How many steps describe how the clay was shaped?

   Write that number here. __________

6. **Write the steps for shaping the clay.**

____

____

____

____

____

____

7. How many steps are used to describe how the clay is fired?

   Write the number here. ______________

8. Is there any step that does not match the three headings: making the clay, shaping the clay, firing the clay?

   Write that step here.

____

____

THINK about what the question asks you to do.

9. **Write the key words again here.**

____

____

____

10. Think about these key words. Think about the information you just wrote to answer the questions in this step. What information will you need for your answer?

Circle the information in Step 2 that you will need for your answer.

WRITE

1. **Write a topic sentence for your answer by completing this sentence.**

My report on Anasazi pottery will be divided _______________

____

____

____

HINT: ***Be sure to include part of the question in this sentence.***

2. **Write the details from Step 2 in the order you want to use them.**

3. **Now write your answer.**

ASSESS *what you have written.*

Now exchange what you have written with a classmate. How do you think his or her answer measures up to this rubric?

4 = I state the main idea clearly.
I include the headings in the correct order.
I include the supporting details that clearly fit under each heading.
I use time-order words correctly to make my answer very clear.
I write complete sentences.

3 = I state the main idea clearly.
I include the headings in the correct order.
I include some details that fit under each heading.
I use a few time-order words.
I write complete sentences.

2 = I state the main idea but not clearly.
I include the headings in the correct order.
I include only a few details that fit under each heading.
I do not use any time-order words.
I write complete sentences.

1 = I do not state the main idea.
I do not include all the headings, or they are not in the correct order.
I include details that do not fit under the headings.
I do not use any time-order words.
I do not use complete sentences.

Before you decide how your classmate's answer scores, let's take a look at a "4" paper.

My report on Anasazi pottery is divided into three headings: making the clay, shaping the clay, and firing the clay. The first part is about making the clay. The clay for making pottery was made by adding sand and water. Sometimes crushed rocks were used. The second part talks about shaping the clay. The Anasazi used the "coil and scrape" method. My report describes the two steps in this method. Firing the clay meant hardening the clay in a fire. This made the clay hard, so the bowl could hold water and food. This is the final part of my report.

What do you think about Yusef's answer?

- ✔ He must have read the question carefully to find out what he was to write about.
- ✔ He repeats some of the key words from the question in the topic sentence.
- ✔ He puts the headings in the correct order.
- ✔ He supports his answer with important details for each heading.
- ✔ He uses time-order words, so his answer reads smoothly.
- ✔ He writes complete sentences.

Let's take a closer look at Yusef's answer to see why it earns a "4".

1. Yusef makes sure he remembers what he is supposed to write about. He uses some of the key words from the question in his topic sentence.

   Write his topic sentence here.

   ____

   ____

   ____

2. Yusef states the three headings and uses details from the article to describe each step.

   Write the two sentences he uses to describe firing the clay pottery.

   ____

   ____

   ____

   ____

3. Yusef uses time-order words in his answer.

   Write one of the sentences in which Yusef uses a time-order word.

   ____

   ____

HINT: ***Notice how these words help connect one idea to the next.***

Skill: Using Descriptive Details

Yusef's answer is interesting because he uses description. But what if someone had not written any description? Read Jean's answer.

My report on Anasazi pottery has three headings: making the clay, shaping the clay, and firing the clay. The first part is about making the clay. The second part is about shaping the clay. The third part is about firing the clay.

This answer is not very interesting. It does not tell you much. And it is also very short. Remember that your answers should fill all or most of the writing lines.

Using descriptive details helps your answers in two ways.

- Description makes your answers interesting. This will help your score.
- Description also helps you fill the writing lines. This will help your score, too.

HINT: ***The description has to be important to the topic.***

4. **Circle two of the following sentences that have descriptions that belong in Jean's answer. Two of the sentences do not fit.**

- The potter scraped the coils with a shell or piece of broken pottery.
- The Anasazi lived in an area we call the Four Corners.
- After the paint dried, the pottery was ready to use.
- A coil is like a series of loops.

Did you use description in your answer? You may want to add more when you revise.

When you have finished assessing your classmate's answer, return it and take a look at what you have written. How did you do?

Look back at Yusef's answer. How does your answer compare to his?

5. Did you repeat part of the question to create your topic sentence?

   If not, try rewriting your topic sentence using some of the key words.

   ____

   ____

   ____

6. Did you include all three headings in your answer?

   If not, write the heading or headings that you left out.

   ____

   ____

7. Did you include at least one descriptive detail about each heading in your answer?

   Circle *yes* or *no*.

8. If you answered no, look back at the article and Step 2. Find descriptive details about the heading or headings that need more description in your answer. Use these descriptions when you rewrite your answer.

   Write the descriptive details you find here.

   ____

   ____

   ____

   ____

   ____

9. If you included descriptive details about each heading, think about whether you want to add some more.

   Underline the place or places in your answer where you might add some more description.

10. Did you use any time-order words in your answer? Would they help to connect your ideas and sentences?

    Circle the place or places where you would add a time-order word.

IMPROVE *your answer.*

1. Think about the ideas you have written down about your answer.
2. Read the rubric again. Will your new ideas give you a "4" paper?
3. **Use your new ideas to revise and rewrite your answer.**

Remember to review the "One Last Look" questions on the next page!

ONE LAST LOOK

Did you

- ❑ answer the question that was asked?
- ❑ include details to make your answer interesting and complete?
- ❑ write complete sentences?
- ❑ fill all or most of the answer lines?
- ❑ check your spelling and punctuation?

Answering Questions That Ask for an Opinion

Lesson 7

Distinguishing Fact From Opinion

A **fact**

- can be proven either true or false, right or wrong.
- can be checked for accuracy (accuracy is whether something is correct or not).

An **opinion**

- is a belief held by a person.
- is what a person thinks or feels about something.
- is based on facts, but is not a fact itself.
- is neither right nor wrong.

Look at these examples to help you understand the difference.

July is a summer month.	July is the best summer month.
This is a statement of fact.	This is an opinion.

See how using the words *the best* changes the statement from a **fact** to an **opinion**? The first statement about July can be proven to be true or false. That July is *the best* summer month is a person's opinion. It cannot be proven to be true or false, right or wrong. It is just how someone feels about July.

To answer a question that asks for your opinion, remember to

- state your opinion in your topic sentence.
- give facts to support that opinion in the rest of your answer.

In this Lesson, you will learn how to...

- answer a question that asks for your opinion.
- use facts to support your opinion.
- write interesting answers by combining sentences.

Rolando, a tenth grader, wrote the following report about year-round schools for his Social Studies class.

YEAR-ROUND SCHOOLS

When you hear the words "year-round school," you probably start to worry. Imagine having to go to school for 12 months out of the year! The idea of not having a 12-week summer vacation may sound awful. But going to school all year isn't as terrible as you may think. Some schools in the United States already have year-round schooling.

Going to school all year doesn't mean you never get a vacation. Students in year-round schools spend the same amount of hours in the classroom as we do. Year-round schools have more breaks during the year. The breaks are just at different times of the year and are shorter than a 12-week summer vacation. Just think. You might be on a schedule that means time off in the middle of winter. You wouldn't have to go to school when it's really cold out. With year-round schooling, that could be possible.

There are two main reasons why year-round schooling is popular. First, research shows that students don't forget as much when they go to school all year. Teachers have compared children who attend school for nine months with children who go to school year-round. When students have long summer breaks, they forget a lot of what they learned the year before. This doesn't happen when school breaks are short.

Second, having two sessions of school all year is a great way to cut class size. Many schools have too many students. It's a fact that students learn better in small classes. Some year-round schools have two sessions. Some students go to school in the morning. Others go to school in the afternoon. Some schools have a lot of students and only a few teachers and not enough classrooms. Year-round schooling works for them. Instead of having 34 students in a classroom, there might be only 17.

As you can see, there are a lot of good reasons to go to school year-round. In fact, I think all students should go to year-round schools.

STEP 1

READ *the question thoughtfully.*

Read the question carefully.

Using information from Rolando's report, explain what you think about year-round schools. Remember to support your opinion with facts from Rolando's report.

1. What are you supposed to do?

   Underline those parts of the question that tell you what to do.

2. **Write those key words here.**

   ____

   ____

   ____

3. Check to be sure you understand what the question asks you to do.

   Restate the question in your own words.

   ____

   ____

   ____

STEP 2

THINK

THINK about what the reading says.

Remember what you learned about facts and opinions on the first page of this lesson. A fact can be checked for accuracy. An opinion is how you feel about something.

1. **Write as many facts from the report as you can.**

2. **Write all the opinions that Rolando gives in his report.**

THINK about what the question asks you to do.

3. **Write the key words again.**

4. What is your opinion of year-round schooling?

   Write your opinion here.

5. Think about the key words and the facts you selected from Rolando's report. Choose the facts that will best explain and support your opinion.

   Circle those facts in number 1 in this step.

WRITE

1. Use the key words and your opinion to create your topic sentence.

   Write your topic sentence here.

2. In Step 2, you wrote and circled facts from the report for your answer.

   Write the facts you circled in Step 2 in the order you want to use them.

3. **Now write your answer.**

ASSESS *what you have written.*

Evaluate your answer against this rubric.

4 = I state my opinion clearly.
I use facts that support my opinion.
I write interesting sentences.
I write complete sentences.

3 = I state my opinion clearly.
I include facts that generally support my opinion.
I write interesting sentences.
I write complete sentences.

2 = I do not state my opinion clearly.
I include only a few facts.
My sentences are mostly simple and uninteresting.
I write complete sentences.

1 = I do not state my opinion. The topic sentence states a fact.
I do not include any facts.
My sentences are not interesting.
I do not write complete sentences.

How does your answer measure up to this rubric? Before you decide, let's look at a "4" paper.

Year-round school would be great. First, it would be great to have more breaks in the year. Sometimes I get bored in the summer. Second, we would remember what we learned because there would be no long breaks. Finally, our school could have two sessions in one day. Then we could have smaller classes. When I am in a smaller class, I learn better. A year-round school could make me smarter.

What do you think about Jillian's answer?

- She has read the question carefully because she answers it with her opinion.
- She states her opinion clearly at the beginning of her answer.
- She uses facts from Rolando's report to support her opinion.
- She writes interesting sentences.
- She writes complete sentences.

Let's take a closer look at Jillian's answer to see why it earns a "4".

1. Jillian clearly states her opinion of year-round school.

Write Jillian's topic sentence that gives her opinion.

HINT: ***Did you notice that Jillian didn't begin her topic sentence with the words I think that? She just started out with her idea. This is one way to have some variety in your topic sentence.***

2. Jillian uses several facts from the report to support her opinion.

   What is the first fact that Jillian uses in her answer?

3. Find another fact Jillian uses to support her opinion.

   Write the sentence that states that fact.

4. Besides the topic sentence, what other sentence has an opinion in it?

   Write that sentence here.

Skill: Combining Sentences

Jillian has written interesting sentences. She has done this by combining sentences.

Short sentences make your writing choppy. Combining short, choppy sentences into longer sentences makes your writing flow more smoothly. Combining sentences also makes your writing sound more natural. You probably do not notice it, but you talk in long sentences.

Let's look at some of the combined sentences in Jillian's answer.

5a. Read the *shorter* sentences below. Then look for the *combined* sentence from Jillian's answer.

Second, we would remember what we learned. There would be no long breaks.

Write the *combined* sentence from Jillian's answer.

____

____

5b. Circle the word Jillian used to combine these two sentences.

5c. Practice sentence combining with these sentences. Remember, you can connect two sentences with a transition word or a punctuation mark.

Combine each pair of sentences.

- Our basketball team played poorly. The other team played worse.

____

- The birds all flew away. The cat crept under the tree.

____

- The fire truck roared around the corner. The people scattered.

____

Are there any short, choppy sentences in your answer? When you revise, think about combining them.

6. Did you notice that Jillian used three time-order transition words in her answer?

   Write the three time-order words here.

   ___

Now let's look at your answer.

7. Did you clearly state your opinion in your topic sentence?

   If not, rewrite your topic sentence here.

   ___

   ___

8. Do all of the facts you used support your opinion? If not, what changes would you make?

   Cross out any facts that do not support your opinion.

9. Would you like to add more facts to your answer? Which ones?

   Write any facts you want to add.

   ___

   ___

   ___

10. Does your answer read smoothly? Or do you have too many short choppy sentences? Reread your answer.

    Underline the sentences you would like to combine when you revise.

STEP 5 IMPROVE *your answer.*

1. Think about the ideas you have written down about your answer.
2. Read the rubric again. Think about your answer and about the description of the "4" paper.
3. **Use all your new ideas to revise and rewrite your answer.**

____

____

____

____

____

____

____

____

ONE LAST LOOK

Did you

- ❑ answer the question that was asked?
- ❑ include details to make your answer interesting and complete?
- ❑ write complete sentences?
- ❑ fill all or most of the answer lines?
- ❑ check your spelling and punctuation?

Lesson 8

Persuading the Reader

To **persuade** means to convince. On a test you may be asked to write a letter or speech to convince someone to give you something or to do something. It doesn't matter if you have to write a speech or a letter. There are three things to remember about writing to persuade people:

- State clearly in your topic sentence what you want.
- Give important reasons to support what you want.
- Stick to the topic.

Stick to the topic means don't throw in unimportant reasons and details. They get in the way of a clear explanation of what you want.

Using specific words can make your writing clearer and more interesting. **Specific words** are words that name a person or thing or describe some action exactly.

- The batter hit a home run.
- The batter slammed it out of the park.

The phrase *slammed it out of the park* is an example of using specific words. You get a clearer and more interesting picture of what happened.

In this Lesson, you will learn how to...

- answer a question that asks you to write a persuasive speech.
- use specific words to make your writing more interesting.

Rayna made the following speech to the city council when a builder wanted to cut down an oak tree to put up an apartment building.

SAVE OUR TREE!

Everyone knows the big oak tree on Second Street. If you try to wrap your arms around it, you can't. We tried and it took four of us to get all the way around it. You can see the roots all the way out by the curb. They made the sidewalk crack and bump up. I think cutting down the tree is a really bad idea for a couple of reasons.

First, the tree is more than 300 years old and it's still alive. There's nothing wrong with the tree. None of the branches are dead. All the branches still grow leaves. If you bend a twig from the tree, you'll see that it's green inside. That is how you can tell the tree is still healthy. Why would anyone kill something that is alive and healthy?

Second, there are a lot of birds' nests in the tree. Where will the birds go if the tree is cut down? Imagine if it were our houses that were going to be taken down to build something else. We wouldn't be very happy about it.

Another reason for saving the tree is that it's a landmark. People say, "Let's meet at the oak tree." Everyone knows where it is. Kids meet there to ride their bikes and skateboards. My friends and I meet there all the time when we go to the movies. Sometimes we just sit on the benches under the tree and talk. If the tree is cut down, where would we meet? We'd have to find some place else to meet.

There are plenty of other places the builder could build an apartment building. There is a vacant lot two blocks away from the tree. There is an empty building next to the gas station on Fourth Street. It could be torn down. It would be better to use up other space in town instead of cutting down our oak tree. I hope that the council doesn't allow the builder to cut down our oak tree.

STEP 1 READ *the question thoughtfully.*

Read the question carefully.

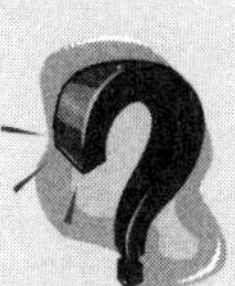

Pretend you are a member of the city council. How would you vote? Explain your decision in writing to the other city council members. You want to persuade them to vote the way you are voting. Use information from Rayna's speech to support your opinion.

1. What are you being asked to write about?

   Now underline those words in the question that tell you what to do. These are the key words.

HINT: ***This question has a great deal of information that you do not need to answer the question. Read through the question and cross out this extra information.***

2. **Write those key words here.**

___

___

___

3. Before you do anything else, make sure you know what to do.

   Restate what the question asks you to do.

STEP 2

THINK

THINK about what the reading says.

1. What is the main idea of Rayna's speech?

   Write the main idea here.

2. What are the most important supporting details for this main idea?

   Write the most important details from the speech that support the main idea.

THINK about what the question asks you to do.

3. **Restate what you are to do.**

   ____

   ____

   ____

4. Before you can persuade anyone else, you have to decide how you would vote. Would you vote to cut down the tree? Or would you vote to save it?

   State how you would vote. ______________________

5. Look back at number 2 in this step. Think about the details you wrote there. Choose the details that you want to use in your answer to support your decision.

   Circle those details.

WRITE

1. You need a topic sentence for your answer.

   Write what you want to convince your fellow city council members to do. This can be your topic sentence.

   ____

   ____

   ____

2. Now, organize your ideas.

   Write the details from Step 2 in the order you want to use them.

HINT: ***Be sure you choose your words carefully. You want to be clear about what you want.***

3. Now you are ready to write what you would say to the city council members.

   Write your answer here.

ASSESS *what you have written.*

Exchange papers with a classmate and read what is written. How convincing is his or her speech? Evaluate it against the following rubric and see.

4 = My decision is stated clearly.
I use details that support my decision.
I use specific words to make my writing clear and interesting.
I write complete sentences.

3 = My decision is stated clearly.
I use details that for the most part support my decision.
I use some specific words.
I write complete sentences.

2 = My decision is not stated clearly.
I include only a few facts, and some don't relate to my decision.
I do not use specific words.
I write complete sentences.

1 = My decision is not stated clearly.
I do not include details that support my decision.
I do not use specific words.
I do not write complete sentences.

How does your classmate's answer measure up to this rubric? Before you decide, let's look at a "4" paper.

I do not think we should chop down the gigantic oak tree on Second Street. First, the tree is very old. Second, it is still alive. Third, many birds make their nests in this sturdy tree. It is their home. Another reason to save the tree is that it is a landmark. People meet under its shady branches. Finally, there are other places to build the apartment house. There is an empty lot two blocks away.

What do think about Maria's answer?

- ✔ She must have read the question, because she answered it completely and correctly.
- ✔ She states her decision in her topic sentence.
- ✔ She supports her answer with important details from Rayna's speech.
- ✔ She uses specific words in her answer.

Let's take a closer look at Maria's answer to see why it earns a "4".

1. Does Maria think the tree should be cut down?

   Write her topic sentence here.

2. **Write one sentence that gives one of the details that Maria uses.**

3. Maria also uses transitions in her answer. She uses five transitions.

   Write her five transitions here.

   ____

Skill: Using Specific Words

One reason that Maria's answer earns a "4" is that she uses specific words. These make her answer more interesting and clearer.

There is no single list of specific nouns, adjectives, or verbs to memorize. But these examples should help you understand what specific words are. They are words that

- name a person or place exactly.
- add excitement and interest to what you write.

General Noun	Specific Noun
person	woman, man, builder, police officer, teacher, Rayna, Maria
house	mansion, cottage, duplex, townhouse, condo
park	Central Park, Redwood National Park, city park

General Adjective	Specific Adjective
big	huge, gigantic, enormous, immense
strong	sturdy, healthy
happy	joyful, delighted, content

General Verb	Specific Verb
say	whisper, yell, scream, shout
cut	slice, chop, trim
move	walk, run, rush, step

4a. Find the specific noun that Maria uses to describe the tree.

Write the noun here.

____

4b. Maria uses three specific adjectives to describe the tree.

Write those three adjectives here.

____

4c. Find the sentence in which Maria uses a specific verb.

Write that sentence.

____

____

When you revise your answer, see if you can replace some ordinary words with extraordinary (specific) words.

After you evaluate your classmate's answer, return it and take some time to look at your own answer. How did you do? How does your evaluator think your answer measures up to the "4" description on the rubric?

5. Did you state your decision about the tree?

Write that sentence here.

____

____

6. Is this your topic sentence?

Circle *yes* or *no*.

7. If you circled no, try rewriting your topic sentence to state your decision about the tree.

   Write your new sentence here.

   ____

   ____

8. Maria has five main supporting details and three important descriptive details in her answer. How many supporting details do you have?

   Write the number here. __________

9. Do you want to add more details to improve your answer?

   Write the supporting details and descriptive details you would like to add.

   ____

   ____

   ____

   ____

10. Did you use any specific words in your answer?

    If you did, circle them in your answer.

11. If you did not use any specific words, would adding some make your answer more interesting? Reread your answer.

    Underline the words you want to replace with specific words.

12. **Write the underline words here that you want to change. Write them in a column on the left side. Next to each one, write a more specific word in the *Specific Word* column.**

General Word	Specific Word

IMPROVE *your answer.*

1. Think about the ideas you have written down about your answer.

2. Read the rubric again. Try to match the description of the "4" paper.

3. **Use all your new ideas to revise and rewrite your answer.**

____

____

____

____

____

____

____

____

ONE LAST LOOK

Did you

- ❑ answer the question that was asked?
- ❑ include details to make your answer interesting and complete?
- ❑ write complete sentences?
- ❑ fill all or most of the answer lines?
- ❑ check your spelling and punctuation?

Part B Testing Yourself

The best way to get ready for a test is to practice. Part 2 gives you six chances to practice the smart way to answer open-ended questions. The six questions are like questions on real tests.

Part 2 has two readings. The first reading is a science article about mistletoe. It is followed by three questions. The second selection is a story. It is also followed by three questions. The number of answer lines should help you decide how much you should write for each answer. If there are eight lines, you should fill all eight.

Use the 5 smart steps to help you.

- Read
- Think
- Write
- Assess
- Improve

Remember to

- follow Steps 1, 2, and 3 to write your answers.
- use Steps 4 and 5 to assess and revise your answers.

Use scratch paper to help you work through the steps.

You have spent time practicing the 5 smart steps. You have the knowledge, you have the skills, you have the tools. You can do it! You can write successful answers.

Dirt? No, Thank You!

Most plants send roots down into dirt. They take in water and nutrients, or food, through the soil. If they are pulled out of the dirt, they cannot live long. But the mistletoe plant is different. This plant's roots do not grow in the ground. Instead, they grow in the trunk or branches of a tree. This plant has learned to survive above ground.

What Does Mistletoe Look Like?

Mistletoe is a yellowish-green plant. It has many little branches and leaves that stay green all year. Many other kinds of plants lose their leaves during the year. The mistletoe's leaves are tough and flexible. They bend like thin leather. Mistletoe leaves may be oval or long and narrow in shape.

The plant's branches grow in a forked pattern. This means many smaller branches shoot out from a main stem. This is a common growth pattern for many plants. The mistletoe's branches can grow up to 2 or 3 feet long. They are droopy. Longer branches hang down instead of standing up.

Late in winter, tiny yellow blossoms appear. Most other plants flower in the spring and summer. Soon after, the mistletoe produces little white berries. These contain seeds. The berries are poisonous if humans and animals eat them.

How Does Mistletoe Get Up in a Tree?

Mistletoe plants grow from their seeds. Most other plants are also grown from seeds, but mistletoe seeds are planted in a special way. The berries are not poisonous for certain birds. The birds are able to eat the berries and the seeds. Because the berry is sticky, a bird may wipe its beak against a tree branch to clean it. Seeds from the berry stick to the bark. When the seeds sprout, they send a root into the tree bark. The root holds the growing plant in place on the tree. The root is like an anchor.

How Does Mistletoe Survive?

The roots of a mistletoe plant take in water and nutrients from the tree. It's as though the mistletoe roots steal from the tree's water and food. In addition, the green leaves of the mistletoe make food by photosynthesis. Photosynthesis is the process by which plants use sunlight and oxygen from the air to make food. Many plants depend on photosynthesis for food.

As you can see, the mistletoe is not altogether like other plants. Dirt? No, thank you! This plant prefers a life high in the air.

Self-Test 1. IDENTIFYING *Main Idea and Supporting Details*

What is the main idea of this science article? Support your answer with details from the article.

Use the following rubric to assess your answer.

4 = The question has been answered completely and correctly.
The answer has a main idea and is clearly organized.
Details are clearly stated and support the main idea.
The writing is interesting and specific words are used.
Transitions are used to make the writing flow well.
Only complete sentences are used.

3 = The question has been answered correctly but not completely.
The answer has a main idea, but is only somewhat organized.
Most of the details support the main idea.
The writing is interesting and specific words are used.
Writing does not always flow easily from sentence to sentence.
Transitions are not used.
Only complete sentences are used.

2 = The question has not been answered completely or accurately.
The answer is not organized and the main idea is unclear.
Most of the details do not support the main idea.
The writing is not interesting and specific words are not used.
Writing does not flow easily from sentence to sentence.
Transitions are not used.
Most of the sentences are complete sentences.

1 = The question has not been answered.
The answer has no main idea and is not organized.
Most of the details are unimportant.
The writing is not interesting and specific words are not used.
Writing is choppy and difficult to read.
Transitions are not used.
Many sentences are not complete sentences.

What score do you give your answer?_______________

How can you improve your writing? On a separate sheet of paper, use the 5 smart steps to revise your answer.

Self-Test 2. EXPLAINING *Steps in a Process*

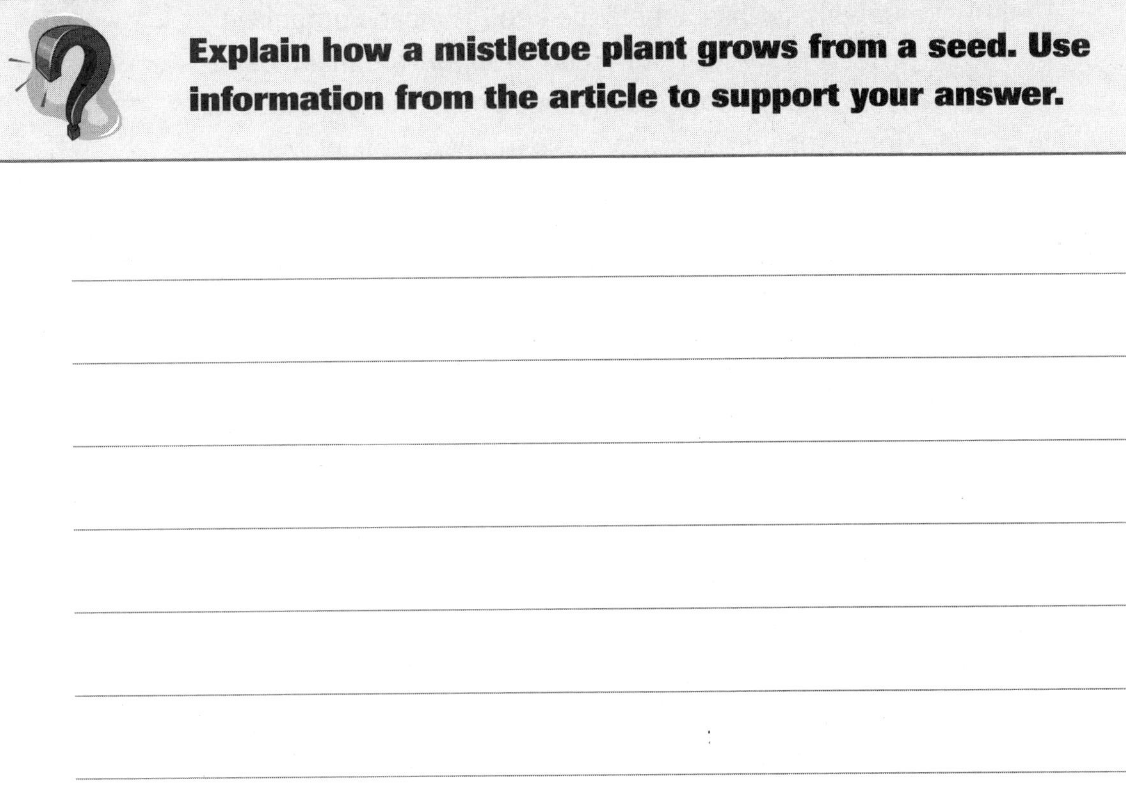

Explain how a mistletoe plant grows from a seed. Use information from the article to support your answer.

Use the following rubric to assess your answer.

4 = The question has been answered completely and correctly.
The answer has a main idea and is clearly organized.
Details are clearly stated and support the main idea.
The writing is interesting and specific words are used.
Transitions are used to make the writing flow well.
Only complete sentences are used.

3 = The question has been answered correctly but not completely.
The answer has a main idea, but is only somewhat organized.
Most of the details support the main idea.
The writing is interesting and specific words are used.
Writing does not always flow easily from sentence to sentence.
Transitions are not used.
Only complete sentences are used.

2 = The question has not been answered completely or accurately.
The answer is not organized and the main idea is unclear.
Most of the details do not support the main idea.
The writing is not interesting and specific words are not used.
Writing does not flow easily from sentence to sentence.
Transitions are not used.
Most of the sentences are complete sentences.

1 = The question has not been answered.
The answer has no main idea and is not organized.
Most of the details are unimportant.
The writing is not interesting and specific words are not used.
Writing is choppy and difficult to read.
Transitions are not used.
Many sentences are not complete sentences.

What score do you give your answer?_______________

How can you improve your writing? On a separate sheet of paper, use the 5 smart steps to revise your answer.

Self-Test 3. COMPARING AND CONTRASTING *Information*

Describe three differences and three similarities between mistletoe plants and most ordinary plants. Use facts from the article to support your answer.

Use the following rubric to assess your answer.

4 = The question has been answered completely and correctly.
The answer has a main idea and is clearly organized.
Details are clearly stated and support the main idea.
The writing is interesting and specific words are used.
Transitions are used to make the writing flow well.
Only complete sentences are used.

3 = The question has been answered correctly but not completely.
The answer has a main idea, but is only somewhat organized.
Most of the details support the main idea.
The writing is interesting and specific words are used.
Writing does not always flow easily from sentence to sentence.
Transitions are not used.
Only complete sentences are used.

2 = The question has not been answered completely or accurately.
The answer is not organized and the main idea is unclear.
Most of the details do not support the main idea.
The writing is not interesting and specific words are not used.
Writing does not flow easily from sentence to sentence.
Transitions are not used.
Most of the sentences are complete sentences.

1 = The question has not been answered.
The answer has no main idea and is not organized.
Most of the details are unimportant.
The writing is not interesting and specific words are not used.
Writing is choppy and difficult to read.
Transitions are not used.
Many sentences are not complete sentences.

What score do you give your answer?______________

How can you improve your writing? On a separate sheet of paper, use the 5 smart steps to revise your answer.

Knock! Knock!

"I miss all my friends back home!" said Trina. Her eyes filled with tears. Mom had said she should give the new town a chance. It would be a great place to live. So far, all Trina felt was homesick.

Mom smiled at Trina. "I know you miss them, honey. But school starts next week. You'll make lots of new friends. You'll see."

That afternoon, Trina lay on her bed feeling lonely. She thought about what Mom had said. She tried to be excited about making new friends. But what she really wanted were her old friends.

Her thoughts were broken by a noise. It sounded like knocking. Was someone knocking on the front door?

The knocking stopped. Then it started again. This time it was in the backyard.

Sliding off the bed, she pushed her feet into her sandals. Then she went through the house into the backyard. The sound had stopped again.

Then—knock-knock! Now the sound was coming from the woods behind her house. What could possibly be making that noise? It sounded like something hard pounding on wood.

Trina crept toward the end of her backyard. What would she find there? She had never lived near woods. She was a city girl. She didn't know what kinds of animals lived in woods. As she walked, she watched for snakes.

Knock-knock! Knock-knock! This time, the noise came from overhead. Trina looked up into the leaves of a large tree.

She was so busy looking into the tree that she didn't see the girl. A girl about her age with brown hair had walked out of the woods.

"It's a woodpecker," she said.

"You startled me," Trina exclaimed.

"Sorry," the other girl said. "That's a woodpecker making the noise. It sounds like a hammer hitting wood."

"I know about woodpeckers," said Trina. "The woodpecker is a bird with a hard beak. It uses its beak to make holes in the sides of trees, where it builds a nest. But I've never seen a woodpecker."

"If you live around here for long, you'll see plenty," said the girl. "Are you?"

"Am I what?" said Trina.

"Living around here."

"Yes," she said. "My mom and I just moved here. I'm starting fourth grade next week."

"That's great," said the girl. "Me, too. My name's Janice. Maybe we can sit together on the bus."

Trina smiled. She had just made her first new friend. It had been easy!

Self-Test 4. EXPLAINING *Cause and Effect*

In the beginning of the story, Trina seems sad. But by the end of the story, she seems happy. What are the causes of Trina's changing feelings? Use details from the story to support your answer.

Use the following rubric to assess your answer.

4 = The question has been answered completely and correctly.
The answer has a main idea and is clearly organized.
Details are clearly stated and support the main idea.
The writing is interesting and specific words are used.
Transitions are used to make the writing flow well.
Only complete sentences are used.

3 = The question has been answered correctly but not completely.
The answer has a main idea, but is only somewhat organized.
Most of the details support the main idea.
The writing is interesting and specific words are used.
Writing does not always flow easily from sentence to sentence.
Transitions are not used.
Only complete sentences are used.

2 = The question has not been answered completely or accurately.
The answer is not organized and the main idea is unclear.
Most of the details do not support the main idea.
The writing is not interesting and specific words are not used.
Writing does not flow easily from sentence to sentence.
Transitions are not used.
Most of the sentences are complete sentences.

1 = The question has not been answered.
The answer has no main idea and is not organized.
Most of the details are unimportant.
The writing is not interesting and specific words are not used.
Writing is choppy and difficult to read.
Transitions are not used.
Many sentences are not complete sentences.

What score do you give your answer?________________

How can you improve your writing? On a separate sheet of paper, use the 5 smart steps to revise your answer.

Self-Test 5. PERSUADING *the Reader*

Choose the part of the story that you think was the MOST important. Pretend you are trying to persuade a classmate to agree with your choice. Use information from the story to explain why you chose that part.

Use the following rubric to assess your answer.

4 = The question has been answered completely and correctly.
The answer has a main idea and is clearly organized.
Details are clearly stated and support the main idea.
The writing is interesting and specific words are used.
Transitions are used to make the writing flow well.
Only complete sentences are used.

3 = The question has been answered correctly but not completely.
The answer has a main idea, but is only somewhat organized.
Most of the details support the main idea.
The writing is interesting and specific words are used.
Writing does not always flow easily from sentence to sentence.
Transitions are not used.
Only complete sentences are used.

2 = The question has not been answered completely or accurately.
The answer is not organized and the main idea is unclear.
Most of the details do not support the main idea.
The writing is not interesting and specific words are not used.
Writing does not flow easily from sentence to sentence.
Transitions are not used.
Most of the sentences are complete sentences.

1 = The question has not been answered.
The answer has no main idea and is not organized.
Most of the details are unimportant.
The writing is not interesting and specific words are not used.
Writing is choppy and difficult to read.
Transitions are not used.
Many sentences are not complete sentences.

What score do you give your answer?_______________

How can you improve your writing? On a separate sheet of paper, use the 5 smart steps to revise your answer.

Self-Test 6. DESCRIBING *a Personal Experience*

By the end of the story, Trina has changed her mind about living in a new town. Think about a time when you changed your mind about something. Describe that experience.

Use the following rubric to assess your answer.

4 = The question has been answered completely and correctly.
The answer has a main idea and is clearly organized.
Details are clearly stated and support the main idea.
The writing is interesting and specific words are used.
Transitions are used to make the writing flow well.
Only complete sentences are used.

3 = The question has been answered correctly but not completely.
The answer has a main idea, but is only somewhat organized.
Most of the details support the main idea.
The writing is interesting and specific words are used.
Writing does not always flow easily from sentence to sentence.
Transitions are not used.
Only complete sentences are used.

2 = The question has not been answered completely or accurately.
The answer is not organized and the main idea is unclear.
Most of the details do not support the main idea.
The writing is not interesting and specific words are not used.
Writing does not flow easily from sentence to sentence.
Transitions are not used.
Most of the sentences are complete sentences.

1 = The question has not been answered.
The answer has no main idea and is not organized.
Most of the details are unimportant.
The writing is not interesting and specific words are not used.
Writing is choppy and difficult to read.
Transitions are not used.
Many sentences are not complete sentences.

What score do you give your answer?_______________

How can you improve your writing? On a separate sheet of paper, use the 5 smart steps to revise your answer.

NOTES

NOTES

NOTES

NOTES

NOTES

NOTES

NOTES

NOTES